John De Vries and Amanda Plummer in a scene from the La Jolla Playhouse production of "Two Rooms." Setting by Marjorie Bradley Kellogg.

TWO ROOMS

BY LEE BLESSING

DRAMATISTS
PLAY SERVICE
INC.

To Jeanne, and to the memory of Jo.

TWO ROOMS received its world premiere at the La Jolla Playhouse (Des McAnuff, Artistic Director; Alan Levey, Managing Director), La Jolla, California, on June 21, 1988. It was directed by Des McAnuff; the set was designed by Marjorie Bradley Kellogg; the costumes were designed by Susan Hilferty; the lighting was designed by Peter A. Kaczorowski; the music was by Michael S. Roth; the sound was by Serge Ossorguine; video production was by Dennis McNabb; and slide photography was by Harry Hendrickson. The cast was as follows:

LAINIE WELLS	Amanda Plummer
WALKER HARRIS	Brent Jennings
ELLEN VAN OSS	Jo Henderson
MICHAEL WELLS	Jon De Vries

A revised version of TWO ROOMS was produced at the Cricket Theater (William Partlan, Artistic Director) in Minneapolis, Minnesota, in October 1989. It was directed by Jeanne Blake; the set design was by Rick Polenek; the lighting design was by Tina Charney; the costume design was by Anne Ruben; and technical direction was by John David Paul. The cast was as follows:

MICHAEL WELLS	Terry Edward Moore
LAINIE WELLS	Camille D'Ambrose
WALKER HARRIS	Steven Hendrickson
ELLEN VAN OSS	Shirley Venard

CHARACTERS

MICHAEL WELLS .... 30's, educator

LAINIE WELLS .... 30's, educator, married to
Michael

WALKER HARRIS.......................... 30's, reporter

ELLEN VAN OSS .... 40's, representative of the
State Department

PLACE

A room

TIME

The recent past, the present

5

TWO ROOMS

ACT ONE

Scene One

Lights rise to reveal a dull-colored emptiness. A narrow mat lies on the floor. The sense of an entry upstage, but no more than that. Michael lies on the mat. He has an unkempt beard, wears a t-shirt and pajamas. He also wears handcuffs. He is blindfolded.

MICHAEL.   Mathison had a gun. Under his jacket. A little automatic pistol or something — I'd never seen it before. Silver. I remember it gleamed in the sunlight when he pulled it out. It was just as they were forcing us both into the car — just as he put one hand on the roof of the car. He was right in front of me, there was nowhere I could go. And suddenly this shining little fantasy pistol appeared. Can you imagine? I taught for two years with the guy and never knew he carried it. As though that was supposed to save us. As though that pitiful gun — that absurd, miniscule tribute to one man's utter lack of realism . . . I mean, he had to know what the world can do — if it just *feels* like it — to a man. To any man. And to carry a gun? The size of a cigarette case? In Beirut? *(He starts to laugh, stops because it hurts.)* He didn't even know what to do once he pulled it out. I think he really believed all those kidnappers would take one look at this mighty weapon of the West, drop their AK-47's and flee. "Run! It's a trap! He's got a tiny gun!" *(Starts to laugh again, stops.)* God, Lainie, I love

7

you. I wish this was a real letter. *(A beat.)* What Mathison forgot was these people have been taking hostages for thousands of years. They know how to do it. He yelled, "I'm armed!" I remember, and that same instant one of them shot it out of his hand, along with some of his fingers, and they slammed us into the car, did the old Kalashnikov-to-the-forehead routine, wrapped Mathison's hand up with his own shirt, blindfolded us and drove us . . . wherever this is. No one spoke. The only sound was Mathison weeping. I wasn't paying that much attention. I was busy counting my own fingers. And toes. *(A beat.)* Ok, this is a digression, but I'm suddenly thinking of your toes. Really. I'm remembering them on the beach at the ocean. First few dates — somewhere in there. You had a bathing suit on — which could have been the first time I saw you in one — and we were lying on towels and you dug your toes down in the wet sand. You dug them around very slowly, and suddenly I felt overwhelmed by this powerful image of . . . a sea turtle, coming ashore, digging in the sand and laying millions, or hundreds — you'd know — of eggs. And it's stupid, but it made me feel connected in a way I'd never felt before, to amphibians. I mean, there they are — forever faced with the choice: go on land and risk their life to lay eggs, or stay in the sea where it's warm and safe and eventually die out. And it occurred to me in that moment that marriage is exactly the same proposition. And I looked at your toes in the sand once more, and . . . married you anyway. *(A beat.)* I wear a blindfold. I can take it off, but if I do they beat me. Or if they come in and it looks re-tied, they beat me. Sometimes it doesn't look like I've taken it off, but since I'm an American they're sure I must have, and they beat me anyway. Their voices are so young. I'm sure it's a delusion, but sometimes I think I've had one or two of them in my class. *(A beat.)* Now I'm in theirs. *(The lights fade quickly to black. When they rise again, Lainie is alone in the room. She stands staring at the empty mat. The room is much brighter — light from an unseen window surrounds her. When she speaks, she addresses the mat at first, then moves around the room. She does not address the audience.)*

LAINIE. I'm talking to myself. All last night, taking the

furniture out of this room, I was talking to myself. It's not the worst habit. Besides, for the last year, what else have I been doing? *(She regards the mat critically, slides it toward one corner of the room, silently appraises its new position.)* Talking to everyone in power — which is, of course, the definition of talking to yourself. I don't know about it here. It'd probably be in a corner, but this one? Which one? *(Sliding it to another corner of the room.)* It's hard to know which was worse: talking to Moslems or talking to Christians. Talking to Lebanese or talking to Syrians. Going across the Green Line to beg, or to Damascus — or Washington. *(Suddenly nods her head decisively.)* Washington. Definitely Washington. The Arabs wouldn't help me, but at least they'd respect the pain. In Washington, I *was* the pain. *(Of the position of the mat.)* This is absolutely wrong. *(She moves it to another corner, stares at it.)* The head of the University said they'd do everything humanly possible to get you back. So did the head of Amal. So did the Lebanese President. So did the Syrian Foreign Minister, our embassy in Beirut, our embassy in Damascus, the Undersecretary of State, the President, and everyone running for President. This doesn't work at all. *(She moves the mat to the center of the room again.)* This is just going to have to stand for all the corners of the room. Why not? It's . . . not an exact science. *(She stares at the mat.)* You'll be here. *(She moves towards the source of light from outside, mimes pulling down a shade and lights dim. She goes to the mat, sits on one side of it, then lies on it, allowing space as though another person were lying on it with her. Tentatively, she reaches out as though stroking the cheek of her 'companion.')* From now on, I'm only talking to you. *(Lights fade to black. When they rise again, Lainie sits on the floor a few feet from the mat, staring at it. Walker stands staring at her.)*

WALKER.   How long has this room been like this? *(A beat.)* Do you redecorate often? *(A beat.)* Rest of the house looks real nice. Very normal. *(A beat.)* This room, though. This room you seem to have done something to. *(A beat.)* Lainie? Can I call you Lainie? *(A beat.)* I want to thank you for letting me come. I know a lot of other reporters would like to be here. I'm glad you chose to talk to me. *(A beat.)* Lainie? *(A beat.)*

So — what is it you'd say you've done to this room?

LAINIE. I cleansed it.

WALKER. Cleansed it? *(Attempting to break the mood.)* Is that a new thing? In decor? Cleansing? *(A beat.)* Lainie? *(A beat.)* It's hard to ask the right questions if you won't —

LAINIE. I scrubbed and painted all the walls. I took all his things out.

WALKER. Was this his room? I mean — is it?

LAINIE. His office. His things were here.

WALKER. Where are they now?

LAINIE. In the basement.

WALKER. What if he comes back? Soon, I mean.

LAINIE. I painted everything. Walls, ceiling.

WALKER. A lot of consistency. What's the mat for?

LAINIE. I look at it.

WALKER. Why? *(A beat.)* Do you mind if I open the shade? *(A beat.)* Lainie? *(Without attempting to open the shade.)* So — does the government keep in contact with you?

LAINIE. She's coming today.

WALKER. She?

LAINIE. The government. Her name is Ellen. She's been attached to me. My case. *(A beat.)*

WALKER. Ellen. What time is she coming?

LAINIE. I liked your voice.

WALKER. What?

LAINIE. Your voice on the phone. I liked it.

WALKER. Why?

LAINIE. It took its time. *(She stares steadily at the mat.)*

WALKER. When is Ellen coming? *(A beat.)* Did you want me to meet her? Is that why I'm here? *(A beat.)* The government hasn't always told the truth on this issue. You do know that. *(A beat.)* I could write about this right now. With what I've got. Just having been here. I could write about this room. What you're saying, what you're not saying. But I won't — if you'll just look at me. *(Again, no response.)* What is it you're staring at?

LAINIE. His hands. *(Lights fade to black. Quickly they fade up again. Ellen now stands where Walker did. Lainie remains in the same position.)*

ELLEN. We think they've moved him. Not far. A different section of town, perhaps. Or even just across the street. We're reasonably certain it's no further than that. It's good strategy for them to move him from time to time. It enhances their power. *(A beat.)* Still, they may have moved him all the way to the Bekaa Valley. That is possible. *(A beat.)* They may not have moved him at all. They may only be pretending to move him. As you know, our intelligence in Beirut isn't the best. Even pretending to move him could enhance their power. *(She sighs.)* Frankly, almost everything enhances their power. It would be hard for Michael's captors to make a mistake, at the moment. Lainie, are you listening to me? *(Walker enters with a small ottoman.)*

WALKER. Here you go.

ELLEN. Thank you.

WALKER. *(Setting it down for her.)* I'm getting your tea. Lainie?

LAINIE. Nothing. *(Walker exits U.)*

ELLEN. Why is he here?

LAINIE. Shouldn't he be here?

ELLEN. He's from a newspaper. What have we been talking about for the last year, Lainie?

LAINIE. It's better to be quiet.

ELLEN. We have no way of knowing what public statements by hostage relatives may do. No way at all. It could make it even harder for us to secure a safe return. I'm disappointed that you called him.

LAINIE. He called me.

ELLEN. I'm disappointed he's here. It's absurd for you to talk to newspapers. Besides, one doesn't talk to newspapers in any case. One lights their fuse. Please, get rid of him.

LAINIE. I can't do that.

ELLEN. *(Starting to go.)* Then I'll go.

LAINIE. No.

ELLEN. I won't be able to be free with information.

LAINIE. When is there ever any information?

ELLEN. *(Sighs, sits.)* When are you going to do something about this room? *(A beat.)* Where were we?

11

LAINIE. You said they were moving him. Or maybe they weren't.

ELLEN. The most important thing to remember is that we're not speaking of a country of terrorists here. We're barely speaking of a country at all. We're speaking of factions. Some friendly to Iran, some to Syria, some to Israel, some to us. They're all fighting for power. For all we know your husband —

LAINIE. Michael.

ELLEN. Michael may be liberated by a faction that favors us. Something like that could happen at any time.

LAINIE. What are the chances?

ELLEN. The important thing is to maintain cautious optimism. Advised hope, I call it. We're hopeful, but we're advised. We're not unintelligent. We recognize the reality of the situation, then we inject hope. Into that reality. Because without hope there can be no foreign policy. *(Walker reenters with a small tray-table. On it is a tea set. He sets it all down next to Ellen and pours.)*

WALKER. I let it steep in the kitchen.

ELLEN. Thank you. *(A beat.)* I'm so odd. Everyone in Washington pumps down coffee all day as fast as they can. And then there's me — with my little cup of tea. I feel like a foreigner. *(She studies the tea a moment.)* The main thing — the crucial thing — is knowing that hope is a real and present possibility. Men have disappeared in Beirut, men have reappeared.

WALKER. So when's Michael Wells going to reappear?

ELLEN. Well — that is what I mean by hope. *(A beat.)*

WALKER. Sorry?

ELLEN. I mean, for example, there are pictures. We have pictures of Michael. Taken just a month ago. Pictures of him alive.

WALKER. He had the shit beat out of him. He was barely recognizable.

ELLEN. The point is, he's alive.

WALKER. He was alive then.

ELLEN. And hope keeps him alive, right up to the present

12

moment. That's why we use hope. Hope enhances our power.

LAINIE.   When will my husband be released?

ELLEN.   We can't say.

WALKER.   What do you mean, you can't say?

ELLEN.   I really should go. I didn't come here for a news conference. *(Ellen moves to leave.)*

LAINIE.   Ellen. *(Ellen stops.)*

WALKER.   It's our Middle-East policy that's keeping your husband hostage. Nothing else.

ELLEN.   That's ridiculous.

WALKER.   In terms of priorities, Michael comes below oil, below U.S.-Soviet relations —

ELLEN.   He's totally uninformed —

WALKER.   Below U.S.-Israeli relations, U.S.-Syrian relations —

ELLEN.   Lainie —

WALKER.   U.S.-*Iranian* relations —

ELLEN.   *(To Lainie.)* You'd be well-advised to reflect on *your* relations with the press.

WALKER.   Can I quote you? *(To Lainie.)* Have you ever wondered why other governments can get their hostages out and we can't?

ELLEN.   They pay ransom.

WALKER.   And it works!

ELLEN.   This government is using every ethical means to bring your husband back to you.

WALKER.   This government wouldn't care if your husband died.

ELLEN.   Mr. Harris!

WALKER.   Because then he's not a problem anymore.

ELLEN.   Either he goes — right now — or I do.

WALKER.   *(To Ellen.)* How does she get you to come out here, anyway? It's a thirty-minute drive.

ELLEN.   Lainie?

LAINIE.   I won't talk to her on the phone.

WALKER.   Really?

LAINIE.   I hang up the minute I hear her voice.

WALKER.   How come?

ELLEN.   Lainie.

LAINIE.   I don't want to be alone when I hear about Michael. I want to hear it from her face to face.
ELLEN.   I come out here because I wish to!
LAINIE.   I told them I'd fast. I'd chain myself to a building.
ELLEN.   We have never taken her seriously.
WALKER.   You're here.
ELLEN.   The Department feels that since Lainie does live close by, and is only asking for one personal visit per week —
LAINIE.   I want two next week.
ELLEN.   One or two visits per week, it's a small price to pay for keeping her —
WALKER.   Quiet?
ELLEN.   From embarrassing herself. You're a newsman, Mr. Harris. Certainly you understand the degree to which media can adversely affect a sensitive situation.
WALKER.   Sure. That's why I investigate every goddamn story I can. *(A beat.)*
ELLEN.   We encounter all sorts of emotional responses in these situations. This we are prepared for. My job is to help victims learn which responses are appropriate, and which are not. The response of running to the papers, in the vain belief that they are somehow the repository of virtue and kindness, is woefully inappropriate. I urge you to ask yourself what's in it for them. *(Starting out, then stopping.)* The government is doing all it can along every avenue. There are however acts of God, for example, over which no government has power.
LAINIE.   You think this is an act of God?
ELLEN.   No. But it is . . . as remote. *(Starting out again.)* I'll be back next Wednesday.
LAINIE.   Monday.
ELLEN.   *(A glimpse of irritation crossing her face.)* Monday. *(Ellen exits U.)*
WALKER.   *(Once she is gone.)* You wonder why the government can't do anything. Right there — that attitude. That's the reason.
LAINIE.   Walker, goodbye.
WALKER.   Goodbye? What do you mean?
LAINIE.   Goodbye.

14

WALKER.   We've just gotten started.

LAINIE.   Goodbye. *(A beat.)*

WALKER.   When can I come back? *(No response.)* You know, I've got better things to do than chase down stories of unco-operative people. *(A beat. He starts to go, stops.)* Do you want me to leave? I'll do what you want me to do. *(A beat.)* Lainie? What is it you want me to do?

LAINIE.   Bring back my husband. *(He stares at her, then leaves. Lights quickly fade to black. When they rise again, Michael is alone onstage, as he was at the beginning.)*

MICHAEL.   I have new guards now. It's been more than a year, hasn't it? They don't tell me exactly. I've discovered some things here. For example, your hands can become friends if they're in handcuffs long enough. *(A beat.)* I once saw a hand just lying in the street. You remember that day I came home, after walking past a car-bombing? I didn't tell you at the time, but I saw it. Just a hand, lying there, unclaimed. It wasn't even horrible so much as . . . terrifyingly lonely. *(A beat.)* I ask myself all the time, "Why did we stay here? Why did we stay here? Why?" *(A beat.)* I look back now and can't believe we stayed. Can't believe we actually sat there at the University and said, "One last term. Then we'll leave." One last term. I wonder if we would've left even then. I wonder if somehow, some part of us even liked the danger. Or was in awe of what we were witnessing. I mean, why does anyone stay? This city's in the hands of boys. Teenagers roam the streets carrying AK-47's and somebody *stays*? I don't know if there's ever been a city that has for this long been such a horror. That's taken itself apart brick by brick, life by life. And so many of us stayed. We walked down the street, through the rubble, past the checkpoints, past the bombings — we had days full of ordinary moments. Amid — what? — devils from Hell. Boys who might shoot you the next moment. Cars that might drive up, park and explode. *(With a growing tension that finally breaks through.)* And none of us seemed ready to say, "Leave it. Let us out of here! Please, *God any*thing but this! *Stop it!!*" *(A beat. He recovers himself.)* And none of us was ever quite ready to leave. *(He moves towards a wall. Lainie enters and sits next to the mat, reaching out as though stroking Michael's hair. Michael is oblivious to her.)*

LAINIE.   Michael? This bothers me. Here on this side, just below your mouth. It's a line here. A little tuck, almost. A wrinkle. It's not on the other side. I don't mind you growing older, but you should do it all over your face, evenly. Don't you think? *(A beat.)* This, though. Here at your temple. I like this. The way the hairs glide along the side, over your ear, into the tangle in back. Just these hairs on the side, running straight back, like they're in a hurry. *(With a slight laugh.)* But all this ear-hair. This has got to go. *(Quieter.)* A beard. I can't imagine it. *(A beat.)* I suppose you don't get enough sleep. Or maybe you do. Maybe all you do is sleep. I hope so. I wish you could sleep from first to last. That you'd never open your eyes again, till I was in front of you. Your eyes are so . . . Why do women love eyes so much? They say it's men that are visual. *(A beat.)* Michael? *(Lights fade to black.)*

Scene Two

A slide appears on the U. wall. It's a picture of a heavily-damaged building in Beirut. We see Lainie and Walker silhouetted on the floor, looking up at it.

LAINIE. This is a hotel in Beirut near where we lived. It was destroyed in some shelling a couple of months before . . . before he was taken. *(We hear the sound of a slide projector. The picture changes: the site of a car-bomb explosion.)* A car bombing. Michael used to take pictures as he walked along. He wasn't looking for these kinds of things. You just couldn't avoid them. People at the University told him it was dangerous. It made people notice him. Even more, I mean. And he did stop a few weeks before . . . *(Another slide: a Lebanese youth, perhaps 15, with an automatic weapon.)* This guy commanded a whole block. He liked Michael. He wanted to pose. *(Another slide: the coast. A few indistinct figures at the shore.)* Michael heard that people had started fishing with grenades. They'd just toss a grenade in the water, and . . . fish that way. *(Another slide: a Lebanese woman, weeping bitterly.)* Michael said he could've taken this picture a hundred times. I'm not sure what it was about her. He didn't know her. He saw something different as he passed. Maybe the sun's shining on her in a different way. Maybe it's something

16

about the way she's standing, or — whatever it is, all the values just seem to . . . hold you. *(Suddenly the projector shuts off. The image disappears. Blackness.)*

WALKER. What's wrong?

LAINIE. I want to stop now.

WALKER. We just started.

LAINIE. I'm sorry.

WALKER. I'll get the lights.

LAINIE. Don't.

WALKER. You want to sit in the dark?

LAINIE. Do you think they still blindfold him?

WALKER. They might. Who can know?

LAINIE. Do they chain him?

WALKER. They might. *(Walker flicks on the lights. He stands at the U. wall. Lainie still sits on the floor.)* Those are good pictures. He's a good photographer.

LAINIE. He's a good teacher, too. I'm sorry. These pictures were harder than I thought. I shouldn't have agreed to show them to you.

WALKER. It's a shame. They'd go awfully well with an interview. If you'd ever give me an interview.

LAINIE. I can't decide.

WALKER. It's been two months. *(A beat.)*

LAINIE. Why haven't you written anything up to now? You have more than enough without me talking.

WALKER. I guess I'd like to have your permission. *(With a self-deprecating laugh.)* My editors think I'm crazy, of course. But that's why. *(A beat.)* I won't write anything if you don't want me to. That's a promise.

LAINIE. What's a promise?

WALKER. You were teaching, weren't you? After you got back here? *(Lainie nods.)* But recently you took a leave of absence?

LAINIE. You've been asking about me?

WALKER. Why'd you leave?

LAINIE. It's hard to teach natural sciences when . . . *(She trails off.)*

WALKER. When what?

LAINIE. When nothing's natural. *(A beat.)*

WALKER. So. Do you sit in here all day?

17

LAINIE.   No. I'm working on a project. It's something I couldn't do in Beirut.

WALKER.   What is it?

LAINIE.   I watch birds. I go down to the marsh a couple miles away, and. . . . Warblers, mostly. I'm working on them.

WALKER.   Does it relax you?

LAINIE.   It teaches me.

WALKER.   And the rest of the time you're in here? Not much of a life. *(A beat.)*

LAINIE.   Michael's here. I can't explain it, but for me he is. In this room. The moment I come in, I feel ... the warmth of his body. The rest of the house — everywhere else — is cold.

WALKER.   You need to talk to people. Away from here. At work, or —

LAINIE.   I work in a marsh.

WALKER.   You should talk to friends. How about the other hostage families?

LAINIE.   It's like looking in a mirror.

WALKER.   Then talk to the public. That really hasn't been tried enough. We could start with an interview. In depth, about —

LAINIE.   My pain?

WALKER.   Among other things. We could run it in the paper. Two, three installments. Maybe more.

LAINIE.   We could run my pain in installments?

WALKER.   It's better than hiding in a marsh. *(A beat.)*

LAINIE.   Ellen says that won't help anyone but the kidnappers.

WALKER.   *No* one knows what will help. That's the first thing. No one knows. All we know is what we've done, and what hasn't worked. Keeping silent hasn't worked.

LAINIE.   Why do you care about this? You don't have anyone over there.

WALKER.   I care about people who are going through what you're going through.

LAINIE.   But why? Why our pain? There's so much to pick from. The world is full of terrible ... outcomes. Why did you choose this? Is it because you can win an award?

WALKER.   An award? What are you talking about?

LAINIE.   Intense suffering. A long series. Lots of installments. A

18

Pulitzer prize.

WALKER. Is that what you think I'm here for? I've been waiting for months! You think that's how I 'd go after a Pulitzer prize? You think I'd wait for you to ask me here? I'd be on your doorstep every day. I'd be out in the marsh with you.

LAINIE. I'm sorry.

WALKER. I've stared into too many faces — yours included — of people who've been told, "Your husband's gone. He may be dead. There's nothing you can do." *(A beat.)* The reason I'm here is because more than anyone this has happened to — any family, I mean — you understand what's really going on.

LAINIE. What's really going on?

WALKER. What's really going on is that they'll let him die. They've already made the value judgment on him and the others. To this administration, it's more effective to use his captivity — and even his death — to push a bunch of policy points, than it is to use every means to get him back.

LAINIE. You really think that?

WALKER. I know it. So do you. The day he's reported dead, do you think they'll be taking any responsibility? They'll be all over TV, pointing the finger at every terrorist in the Middle East and saying, "These are barbarians. Don't try to understand them, just let us do what we must do." And we'll let them.

LAINIE. What do you think I should do?

WALKER. I've said. Speak out. Do interviews. Go on TV if you have to. *(She considers this.)*

LAINIE. No.

WALKER. Why not?

LAINIE. *(Shakes her head.)* It's too public for me. It's too . . . public.

WALKER. Well. Fear of speaking. Right up there with — what? Fear of falling, fear of loud noises —

LAINIE. That's not fair.

WALKER. Oh, I'm not being fair? Sorry. You're right. Loud noises can be pretty rough. *(He suddenly claps his hand loudly behind her ear. She pulls away from it, holding her ear in pain.)*

LAINIE. *Stop* that!

WALKER. That's probably going to be the last thing Michael ever hears. Only it won't be two hands clapping, it'll be a gun.

19

LAINIE.   Get out of here!

WALKER.   Care about your husband.

LAINIE.   I do!

WALKER.   Do something!

LAINIE.   I *am*!

WALKER.   Do more!

LAINIE.   *No!!* (*A beat.*) You know what will get him back? Nothing we can understand. Whatever took Michael, whatever will bring him back is a power so incomprehensible we'll never understand it. And all the running around screaming about injustice won't change a thing. All we can do—all *any*one can do —is take pictures of mourning widows. Write stories about mourning widows. Become fascinated with widows of men who aren't even dead yet. But nothing — *nothing* — will make a difference.

WALKER.   Lainie, I'm only —

LAINIE.   Get out! If I want to see a scavenger, I'll go to the marsh. (*A beat. Walker hesitates, then exist. Lights fade to black. When they rise again, Michael sits alone on the mat. He is blindfolded.*)

MICHAEL.   (*A beat.*) War isn't a tear in the fabric of things, it is the fabric. If earth is our mother, our father is war. The chief priority we have on earth is to vie with each other for a place to stand. Does any of this make sense, Lainie? I'm trying to explain why this has happened to us. Americans fight all the time — lots of wars. But always far away. We haven't had to fight for the soil we stand on in a century. We've forgotten that level of sacrifice. These people haven't. Everyone in this country — Christian, Sunni Moslem, Shi'ite, Palestinian, Israeli — everyone is fighting for the ground. The ground itself. They stand here or nowhere. So it's easy for them to give up their lives. Small sacrifice. It's easy for them to kill, too. Small sacrifice. You know how being here, being swallowed up by it, makes me feel? Like I'm finally part of the real world. For the first time. Lainie, something in me never felt . . . affected . . . until this happened. You know what it makes me think of? Shiloh. Vicksburg. The Wilderness. What those places must have been like: suffocating, endless, bleeding disaster. Stacking of bodies ten deep for a few feet of *our ground*. Don't you see? We're not different from these people, we've just forgotten. We think this urge doesn't exist anymore. We abstract everything, we objectify. We talk about global politics, how all this affects the balance of power. Do you know what a twenty-year-old Shi'ite thinks of the balance of power? *(Lights fade to black.)*

Scene Three

Lights fade up to reveal Ellen sitting in a chair. Lainie sits on the floor facing her.

ELLEN. I got a call today.

LAINIE. About Michael?

ELLEN. Not exactly. About Walker. He's been visiting you now and then, hasn't he?

LAINIE. What's wrong with that?

ELLEN. Nothing. He was here about a week ago. You looked at slides, I believe.

LAINIE. How do you know that? Did he tell you?

ELLEN. Walker? Oh, no. *(Laughs slightly.)* No, no, no. Sometimes we watch your house.

LAINIE. You do?

ELLEN. Of course. You're on the list.

LAINIE. What list?

ELLEN. The Watch Your House list. You've made threats. You're a potential embarrassment. In the realm of international politics, that can be serious. Terrorists can use what you do. What Walker does, too. Americans are often naive in their efforts to affect things like the media, public opinion. They can end up helping this country's enemies far more than themselves. In a situation like this, where so little can be done, the temptation must be irresistible to do something irrational, counterproductive. That's the only way I can understand what Walker's done.

LAINIE. What's he done?

ELLEN. Oh, that's right. You don't know yet. That call I got? It was from one of his editors. Walker's written a story. About you. It'll be out tomorrow. Not an interview. He doesn't quote you directly. But he details the kidnapping, and all your various meetings with people during the early months, and . . . I'm afraid

21

. . . also this room.

LAINIE.   He'd never do that without telling me.

ELLEN.   That's what I thought. That's why I'm here, in fact. To find out if he really has done this behind your back. *(A beat.)* Is that the case?

LAINIE.   Can we get them not to print the story?

ELLEN.   No. But I'd like to make a suggestion or two, if I could.

LAINIE.   What?

ELLEN.   If you were to make a public statement disavowing the article, that might help. Perhaps having a different reporter, from a newspaper we could recommend, come in and see this room in a more normal state —

LAINIE.   No.

ELLEN.   Whatever you like. Perhaps only a photographer. Just a picture of you sitting in this room with furniture, the window open . . . *(Lainie is silent.)* Well. Let's see what damage is done before we look for solutions. *(A beat. Ellen rises.)* I probably should be getting back to the office. *(She moves to leave. Lainie is motionless.)* Lainie? Are you all right?

LAINIE.   Are you pretending to care?

ELLEN.   I care very much. I think you know that.

LAINIE.   If you did, you'd do something.

ELLEN.   I told you, there's nothing we can do about Walker —

LAINIE.   Not about Walker; about Michael.

ELLEN.   We do things all the time. Every day. We just can't tell you about them.

LAINIE.   Nothing happens.

ELLEN.   Sometimes something happens. People do get released.

LAINIE.   Not because of anything you do.

ELLEN.   You can't know that.

LAINIE.   I can't know much, given how little you tell me.

ELLEN.   A government must have secrets.

LAINIE.   Why?

ELLEN.   I'm not conducting a course for children. *(A beat.)* We need silence. From you, from all the hostage families. And a willingness to let us do our job. It isn't easy for you, we know that. But talking with people like Walker doesn't help anyone, and as we've learned today, it's its own punishment. The one thing you can do — the only thing that will be of any use — is to hope.

LAINIE. Hope?

ELLEN. Hope.

LAINIE. Hope doesn't come from you, does it?

ELLEN. What do you mean?

LAINIE. It comes from God, doesn't it? Or Allah? Jehovah? Fate? A higher power — isn't that right? Certainly not the government. The government doesn't dole out hope. It's not an entitlement program.

ELLEN. I don't see how this —

LAINIE. I study hope all the time. You know where? The marsh. I watch the warblers there, nesting. I know their whole life cycle. Little, friendly I-won't-bore-you-with-the-Latin-name warblers. Thousands of them. Going about their business. Not too many predators, plenty of insects to eat. They wouldn't need hope at all if it weren't for one thing.

ELLEN. Which is?

LAINIE. The cuckoo. A much larger bird. Fewer of them, but . . . larger.

ELLEN. I'm not sure I see the connection.

LAINIE. You're right. Cuckoos don't eat warblers. They also eat insects. But cuckoos don't build nests. Instead, they wait till the warblers are away from theirs. Then they lay their eggs in the middle of all the warbler eggs. Neat, eh? Camouflage.

ELLEN. Sounds . . . effective.

LAINIE. Oh, it works every time. The warblers return, and because they have — literally — bird brains, they don't seem to notice the great big egg among the little ones. They sit on them all. And what do you think happens? I mean, what's evolution for? The cuckoo hatches first. And there he is — nearly as big as his step-parents, demanding an immense volume of food, and waiting for the warbler eggs to hatch one by one. And when they do, do you know what happens then?

ELLEN. Inform me.

LAINIE. They crawl around — blind, as the cuckoo chick is blind — in the nest, waiting for their parents to return with food. But as they do, one by one, they encounter a miracle of natural selection: the back of the baby cuckoo.

ELLEN. The back?

LAINIE. Its back, unlike other birds' backs, is indented. There's a hollow. And you know what it's shaped like? What it's just big enough for? A baby warbler. And yet another miracle of nature: the baby cuckoo has an instinct. To do what? Push against anything that touches its back. Push and push until that thing is not there anymore. And with great effectiveness, one by one, this blind, newborn, totally innocent bird murders each of the blind, newborn, totally innocent warblers, by pushing them out of the nest where they'll starve or be eaten by rats and snakes.

ELLEN. Thank you for sharing such a wonderful story.

LAINIE. I'm not done. Warbler Mom and Dad come home. What do they find? One baby — which is as big as a Buick, and doesn't chirp like them. What do they think? Who will ever know? What do they do? Feed the only baby they have. Until one day it flies off, fully-fledged, a different species. And God or Allah or Nature or Fate — which we've already agreed is the author of hope — looks on with something more than indifference. With approval. *(A beat.)* The indentation in the cuckoo's back — that is the face of God. That is the chance of hope in the world.

ELLEN. Not every nest is visited by a cuckoo.

LAINIE. Mine was. Now offer me hope. *(Lainie turns, exits quickly U. Ellen sighs, starts to follow after her. Before she can reach the door, Michael enters, in handcuffs. He is blindfolded. Ellen is unsurprised to see him.)*

MICHAEL. They take me to the bathroom once a day. If I'm lucky I can shower once a month. Pardon my appearance.

ELLEN. That's perfectly all right.

MICHAEL. I imagine you dream about all your hostages.

ELLEN. Just you.

MICHAEL. Really?

ELLEN. Well, I'm assigned to you. The State Department is very big. Other hostages are dreamt about by others.

MICHAEL. *(Nods.)* Ah.

ELLEN. Don't misunderstand. The dreams don't bother me.

MICHAEL. They don't?

ELLEN. What do you . . . think about all day?

MICHAEL. I think about a man as a stored object. As a broom in a broom closet. I think about brine shrimp in the Kalahari.

ELLEN. Brine shrimp?

MICHAEL. Tiny shrimp that live in the desert, in Africa. Lainie told me about them. They can live for years in suspended animation in the mud of a dry lakebed. When rain comes — if it comes — they wake up, and swim around, and procreate as fast as they can and get eaten by everything around them. Then after a week or two the lake dries up again, and the lucky ones hit the mud for another . . . decade. Ninety-nine percent of their life is spent waiting for their life. You get out of the United States, you see a lot of that. Whole cultures waiting to be alive.

ELLEN. You're sympathetic to your captors' cause. The Stockholm Effect. A common syndrome — it's documented.

MICHAEL. It's convenient. You're sure your dreams don't bother you?

ELLEN. No more than the student's dream of being late to the exam bothers the student. There's some real anxiety at first, but ultimately —

MICHAEL. Indifference?

ELLEN. I realize it's not real.

MICHAEL. I am real.

ELLEN. Of course. But I'm not required to treat you that way. (She exits quickly U. Lights fade to black.)

Scene Four

Lights rise to reveal Lainie and Walker. The chair is gone.

WALKER. I want to be able to give you my side of things. (A beat.) I want to show you that what I did —

LAINIE. You promised me. (A beat.)

WALKER. That what I did —

LAINIE. You promised me.

WALKER. Lainie —

LAINIE. This room. You put this room in a newspaper.

WALKER. It's in a newspaper every day. It's Michael's room. It's the room they're all in. Hell, everyone's in it. We can't get out.

LAINIE. People call me. They've been calling all week. They want to know if this room really exists. They want to know if they can come over.

WALKER. I'm sorry.

LAINIE. You're sorry?! My life hasn't been that different, you know. I've had friends take advantage of me before. I've had them hurt me, betray me. I know what it's like. But I never thought someone would come into my life now — as it is now — and do this.

WALKER. Lainie —

LAINIE. *Why!?*

WALKER. 'Cause you were smothering, that's why. You were sitting in here and pumping the air out, and for all Washington cared you could do it forever. Your husband, the men in Lebanon, the people in this country need you. They need you to say "I hurt" — in public. They need you to say, "I don't believe my government," and "We have to try new ways." They need to hear you say it over and over.

LAINIE. *That's for me to decide! That's my choice! You took my choice!* (*A silence.*) You think that just because you've been in this room, you understand it? It's the one place I can go and find Michael. Where I can feel — however imperfectly — what he's experiencing. No barrier between us. No one coming between. No one. I don't have to hear about him from a government spokesperson, or a reporter or concerned friends — I have him here. He's mine.

WALKER. (*Quietly.*) It's an illusion.

LAINIE. *What isn't?* How do you want me to experience Michael? On the news? In the faces of all the sick human beings I've had to beg for his freedom? Holding hands with how many other helpless relatives? You're a great one to talk about illusions — that's your whole business. If I can have Michael — no matter how I do it — I'm going to have him. Do you understand?

WALKER. Lainie —

LAINIE. *Do you understand?!* (*A beat. Walker nods, turns to leave.*) People are calling me. Reporters — other reporters — want to do articles about me and this room. What are we going to do about that?

WALKER. I don't know. I'm sorry. (*A beat. He starts out again.*)

26

LAINIE. I'm going to give you an exclusive interview.

WALKER. Why?

LAINIE. Because now that you've written what you've written, talking to someone is inevitable. Unless I just want to be thought of as . . . odd, I'll have to speak out. A lot of reporters would work, I suppose. But with you there's a special advantage. I know how far I can trust you. *(Walker exits. Lights fade quickly to black and quickly rise again. Lainie is with Michael, who is blindfolded.)*

MICHAEL. Some days I go around a room at home. Any room. Doesn't matter, they're all wonderlands compared to where I'm kept. Today it's my office. I try to remember everything about every piece of furniture. Where I bought it, what it was like that day, the smells in the air. It's really very sobering, how much the mind recalls when it's forced to. I remember my chair, my filing cabinet — and not just my filing cabinet, but the exact order of files: household, course-plans, medical, automobile, retirement — all of it. As if I took a picture. I remember the *smell* of my desk. And each day. I think I remember each day in my office — all of them. Cold days, wet days, days of incredible light. *(A beat.)* Did I tell you I was making a new country? On the wall. I feel the tiny bumps. They're mountains, of course. And the cracks are rivers. I work on it all day, sometimes. Every mountain has a name. There's Mount Freedom — of course. There's Mount Hope and Mount Sense of Humor. And Mount Forgiveness. There's Mount Forgiveness. Most days though, I fill up with the people we know. You, mostly. *(Lainie carefully removes Michael's blindfold. He smiles at her.)* You know that child we thought about having? We had him. He's um . . . almost six months now. I'm aging him faster than normal so we can talk together sooner. His name is Andrew. Because I like it. He has your hair and eyes, and . . . I can't tell about his nose yet. We may have a daughter later, I'm not ruling it out. *(A beat. They stare at each other.)* Who can predict the future? *(Lights fade quickly to black.)*

END OF ACT ONE

ACT TWO

Scene One

A tight spot comes up on Ellen, sitting on a chair in the room. She smiles.

ELLEN. What does it mean to be an American? Well, here it means — for most of us — "to be comfortable." Elsewhere in the world it means to be punished. To be punished justly, some would say, for the crime of having been born here and not there. *(We suddenly see a slide of a young Shi'ite terrorist on the same wall Lainie's slides appeared in Act One.)* This is one of those who does the punishing. He may be college-educated. He may well be a graduate of the American University in Beirut. He may be a shepherd, with no education whatsoever. He may speak English, or only Arabic. He may be devout — he may not. He may be utterly committed to his cause, or only doing this because it provides work and food and some measure of security. Perhaps he likes the excitement. Perhaps, like most young men, he just likes the guns. He may be relatively humane; he may be monstrous. *(Another slide — another young Shi'ite terrorist.)* Here's another one. *(Another slide — another young Shi'ite terrorist.)* And another. *(Another slide — another young Shi'ite terrorist, then several more in quick succession. She speaks as they flash past.)* And another, and another, and — thousands in this country. And this of course is only one country. Think of it — enormous numbers of people all over the world hating Americans. Hating other Westerners too, of course, but particularly Americans. Willing to kill even the most innocent of us. To make an example of our men, women, children, infants, of the aged, the infirm — of *any* American. To imprison us without trial. For years. Why? *(Another slide — a very young Shi'ite terrorist, complete with rocket-launcher.)* They watch our television, you know. See our films, wear our clothes, drive our cars, listen to our music. They use our technology — what they can afford of it. They learn in our universities. What do they learn? That by sheerest accident, they have been born in a part of the world which has no power. That to be an uneducated person in a small country, speaking a bypassed language, worshipping an old-fashioned god is worse than death. That to be such a person without a *revolution* — or promise of a revolution — is to be shut in a room, blindfolded, with a chain around your ankle for life. *(More slides — pictures of slain hostages William Buckley, Peter Kilburn and William Higgins.)* These men are dead. They were American hostages taken in Lebanon, and later apparently murdered. They were not killed for who they were so much as for who they might have been: that is, any of us. They were our representatives in death. Their lives were erased by those whose lives otherwise might never have been written. *(Another slide — Shi'ite militiamen celebrating in a Beirut street.)* Men whose only reality is to reject and destroy what they can of the Western world — which floats before them as an unreachable illusion, both detested and desired. Infinitely powerful, infinitely weak. In a real sense, the Crusades are here again. We in the State Department understand that. It's our job to be ready to sacrifice the few for the many when necessary, and we do. It's our job to look down the road, to ascertain what is and isn't likely to happen, and form our judgments accordingly. For example. *(More slides: Americans who have been kidnapped in Lebanon since 1984.)* These men, all kidnap victims, are of course undergoing dehumanizing conditions in their false imprisonment. No one denies this. They are being held by men who would as soon kill them as anything else. Yet, since 1984 out of the total of more than sixty foreigners taken, only a few have died. Over thirty have been released. We in State have to believe that the kidnappers are no more interested in dead hostages than we are. We have to believe that time is therefore on our side, not theirs. That ultimately the situation will be resolved — after a presidential election here, or a shift in the military or political situation there or whatever. A break will come. *(The slides stop on a picture of Peter Kilburn.)* But if I'm wrong, if these men in fact all suffer torture and die as a direct result of this country's policy in the Middle East, I must be ready to accept that too. American citizens have to realize that when we take a risk, the U.S. government can't always save us. That the time comes when we — on an individual basis — will simply have to pay. *(The slide goes out. Total blackness. When lights rise again, Lainie and Michael sit on the mat in the same position as at the end of Act One.)*

LAINIE.   Do they move you very often?

MICHAEL.   Now and then.

LAINIE.   Are the rooms ever different?

MICHAEL.   It's always the same room. Whatever it looks like.

LAINIE.   Why do they move you?

MICHAEL.   They're nervous. I'm a prize, remember? The Army could steal me away, another faction could steal me. Sort of like sea gulls fighting over an orange rind on the beach.

LAINIE.   What do you do all day?

MICHAEL.   Write letters to you. What do you do?

LAINIE.   Well, I . . . I do a lot of things. I do my work.

MICHAEL.   And how's that?

LAINIE.   Oh, you know . . . never-ending.

MICHAEL.   *(With a smile.)* That's the trouble with nature. What else do you do?

LAINIE.   Nothing.

MICHAEL.   Still?

LAINIE.   I'm still getting used to it.

MICHAEL.   It's been a —

LAINIE.   I know how long it's been — it's been longer than my life, all right?

MICHAEL.   I know.

LAINIE.   I wish they kidnapped women.

MICHAEL.   They do. Sometimes.

LAINIE.   They let them go. *(A beat.)*

MICHAEL.   Does anything make you happy?

LAINIE.   Sometimes Walker does.

MICHAEL.   What's he like?

LAINIE.   He's like you. He likes to be where he's told he shouldn't be. *(A beat.)* I gave him an interview.

MICHAEL.   You did?

LAINIE.   I talked about you. I talked about how little anyone's doing. All the standard things. I feel like such a fool when it's all over and nothing's happened. We all of us seem that way to me sometimes — all the ones who speak out. Going around the country, grabbing the whole nation by the elbow, saying, "Please? Can't you do something?" *(A beat.)* Do you ever hear gunfire where you are? Or shelling?

MICHAEL. Yes.

LAINIE. Close?

MICHAEL. Close enough. I fantasize sometimes that the place gets hit. A hole opens up, and I run out of it. Like someone escaping from a crashed plane. About the same odds, I suppose. I like the room this way. Thanks.

LAINIE. Ellen always want me to open the window.

MICHAEL. Maybe you should.

LAINIE. You think so?

MICHAEL. You know what I'd give for a window?

LAINIE. Yes. *(He rises, moves towards the window. He makes a gesture as though opening a curtain. Light pours into the room. He looks out, smiles. Lainie rises and joins him at the window. After a moment Michael exits U., leaving Lainie staring out. Lights fade to black. When they rise again, Ellen and Lainie stand across the room from each other. The light in the room window is apparently still open, since the light remains brighter.)*

ELLEN. Well. This is certainly an improvement.

LAINIE. Thank you.

ELLEN. When did you start opening the window?

LAINIE. A couple of weeks ago. Right after you were here last.

ELLEN. Really. It's much more pleasant. Maybe I should stay away longer next time.

LAINIE. If you do, don't come back.

ELLEN. Don't be cross. You know I've had to be in the office every minute lately. That's the whole point of a crisis, isn't it? Keep the bureaucrats in their place.

LAINIE. How's the crisis coming?

ELLEN. You should know. You're doing enough to intensify it.

LAINIE. That's not what I'm doing.

ELLEN. It isn't? Let me remind you of your phone call to me yesterday.

LAINIE. You don't have to —

ELLEN. *(From memory — perfectly, of course.)* Walker says I should go on TV. I think he may be right. Maybe this is a real opportunity to put pressure on people.

LAINIE. I didn't mean you.

ELLEN. Of course you meant me. You meant the State Department.

31

LAINIE.   All right, so I did mean you. So what?

ELLEN.   Lainie, this crisis has been manageable so far. But there's no telling what can happen. We have a lot of Americans trapped with some exceedingly dangerous terrorists in a very cramped charter terminal in Crete. If you and other hostage relatives start jumping onto TV screens now, God knows what effect it will have.

LAINIE.   Maybe a good effect.

ELLEN.   I doubt it. Lainie, there are twenty-three American lives in that building. We can't break in, they have the building rigged to explode. We have to bargain. Fast. It's important that no other issue gets involved.

LAINIE.   You mean Michael.

ELLEN.   We're speaking of innocent lives here.

LAINIE.   What's Michael? Guilty?

ELLEN.   *(With a frustrated sigh.)* There's a dead serviceman lying twenty feet from the door of that terminal. At the moment they won't even let us take his body away.

LAINIE.   I know.

ELLEN.   He just thought he was on vacation. He wasn't even in uniform. But he was unfortunate enough to have a military I.D., and —

LAINIE.   *I know. (A beat.)* Can't we just wait them out? Can't we — ?

ELLEN.   This group likes to die for what they believe in. They're not like a bunch of bank robbers. As far as they're concerned, when they die, they win. *(A beat.)* Now, they *have* made demands. They want some fellow terrorists released. Those demands are being studied by various . . . governments, and just between you and me, we may be able to come to an agreement. Or somebody may. It's rather complicated, you can imagine. But believe me, when terrorists take a group as large as this, everyone understands it's a short-term project.

LAINIE.   Project? Is that how you see it? What's Michael — a long-term project?

ELLEN.   Sadly, in a sense, yes.

LAINIE.   Because he wasn't lucky enough to be abducted in an airport? With a bunch of other people?

ELLEN.   Lainie, there are physical realities.

LAINIE. What about moral realities?

ELLEN. Please — don't mix apples and oranges. If you go public, if you make demands, you'll only delay matters and increase the danger for everyone involved. And frankly, no matter what you do, we won't ask for Michael's release.

LAINIE. You won't?

ELLEN. It's not his time.

LAINIE. His *time?*

ELLEN. It's nice with the window open. You should leave it this way, I think. *(Rising to leave.)* Well. I don't have much free time. I'm afraid I'll only be able to talk on the phone, at least until this present emergency's over. It's hard for me to be away right now. Lainie? *(Lainie hasn't moved.)* Soon it will be over and everything will be back to normal. *(A beat.)* I *am* sorry it can't be now. *(Ellen exits. Lights fade to black, then quickly rise again on Walker entering with a photograph in his hand.)*

WALKER. *(Calling out loudly.)* Lainie! This is great! This is fantastic! Thank you!

LAINIE. *(Entering.)* It's just a picture.

WALKER. Are you kidding? Michael and Jim Mathison together at the University of Beirut? You never told me you had this.

LAINIE. I didn't see any reason to —

WALKER. Look at it. They've got their arms around each other, they look warm, human, vulnerable — it's perfect.

LAINIE. Walker —

WALKER. We've got to bring this along. They'll want to use it on the show, I know it.

LAINIE. You think so?

WALKER. They'd kill for it. It's got everything you'd want: simple, affecting — this'll communicate.

LAINIE. I don't want to bring it.

WALKER. You don't?

LAINIE. I look at that picture. I don't want it flashed all over the country.

WALKER. Why not? That's exactly what you want to do. It's the perfect one. It affects you. It'll affect other people. *(She takes it from him.)*

LAINIE. I'll find another one.

WALKER. No.

LAINIE. No?

WALKER. Either you're going to do this or you're not. You have a chance to make a statement here. But it's only going to be heard if you make it as strong as possible. "Quietest Hostage Wife Speaks Out" is a headline. "Quietest Hostage Wife Sort Of Speaks Out" isn't.

LAINIE. But this is a picture.

WALKER. Doesn't matter. It's all imagery. The pictures we choose, the copy we write, the interviews you give — it's all a matter of giving the proper image. That's how people think. Images — not ideas. Images.

LAINIE. *(Of the picture.)* If I give this up, I give it up. I won't be able to look at it. *(A beat. She gives it to him.)*

WALKER. Good. Thanks. They'll pick this up everywhere, believe me. They'll run it all over — all the networks. This is the perfect time. Couldn't be more perfect. I was afraid this would all be over by now, I really was.

LAINIE. Have they let anyone go? Women, children?

WALKER. Nobody. Not a one.

LAINIE. What if they decide to . . . to — ?

WALKER. Kill more of them? It's possible. But it's not all that likely. They've already made their point with the soldier. We know they're serious.

LAINIE. They could get nervous. Someone could make a mistake.

WALKER. No one's going to make a mistake. These things are rituals. Everyone knows the role they're playing. Our role is to get Michael into the deal. We can, too. We're going to help him — starting with this . . . *(Indicates the picture.)* and one very intense interview. Come on — let's get you down to the studio. *(He moves to leave, turns, sees that she's not moving.)* Come on.

LAINIE. What happens after the interview?

WALKER. Another interview. Maybe a lot of them.

LAINIE. And after that?

WALKER. Everybody. Everybody who asks. 7 o'clock, 11 o'clock, late-night news shows. You name it.

LAINIE. And after that?

WALKER. I don't know. Threatening phone calls from the State

Department — or the White House, if we're lucky.

LAINIE. And from the families of the new hostages. They're going to hate me — you know that, don't you? If I try to complicate this negotiation by insisting that Michael —

WALKER. Bullshit.

LAINIE. It's not bullshit. They will.

WALKER. Do you care?

LAINIE. Of course I care. I know what they're going through —

WALKER. How long have they been going through it? *(A beat.)* You've been in line. It's your turn, too — not just theirs. *(Michael enters, handcuffed but not blindfolded. Walker is oblivious to him, but Lainie sees him. Michael smiles at her, goes and lies down on the mat, closing his eyes.)*

LAINIE. All right.

WALKER. *(Taking her by the hand, exiting.)* Come on. Believe me, you'll get used to it. *(They exit. Michael suddenly bolts straight up, screaming.)*

MICHAEL. *LAINIE!! LAINIE!! (A beat. He looks around fearfully, as though expecting someone to enter. When no one does, he relaxes slightly.)* They moved me again. That's why I dreamed. They have a box that they put me in when they move me. It's the shape of a coffin. And it's soundproof. The first time they tried it, they put the box in the back of a van with a bad exhaust system. I was unconscious when they took me out. I know this is an illusion, but sometimes — usually right in the middle of the night — it occurs to me that I don't know, I don't absolutely *know*, whether I'm alive or dead. *(A beat.)* They brought Mathison here — you know that? No, of course you don't. I never actually saw him. They moved him into a room just down the hall. I could hear him go by once a day when they took him to the bathroom. He said something in the hall the first time he passed by. They shouted at him to shut up, but I could tell his voice. I was afraid they'd take him away again if I said anything back. I'd been warned about that sort of thing before. So for a week I'd just listen to him shuffle past, once a day. Then one day, I heard them moving him — for good, I thought — so I shouted to him. "Mathison!" Once, real loud. It got very silent in the hall. Then the sound of them shoving him out, and then my door opened. Two guards came into my room and beat me. They never would admit

35

he'd been there. But I knew. I heard him. He heard me. *(Lights fade out on Michael.)*

Scene Two

Lights up on the empty room. Walker enters carries a glass of champagne. He calls out.

WALKER.   Hey, Lainie! Come in here! What are you doing?

LAINIE.   *(Off.)* I'm getting some coffee.

WALKER.   Coffee?

LAINIE.   *(Off.)* We need to sober up.

WALKER.   Why!? We did it! We got the message out! We put those bastards on the spot. They're going to have to ask for everybody — I know it!

LAINIE.   *(Entering with a cup of coffee.)* I can't remember the last time I had alcohol.

WALKER.   *(Holding his glass towards her.)* Have some more. I'm sure it's a very good month.

LAINIE.   No, thanks. This'll be fine. *(Gradually a silence surrounds them. They look at each other, can't help a smile and a slight laugh.)*

WALKER.   You were fantastic. Fantastic. Everybody in America felt for you. And that picture. Was I right or what? The cameramen were tearing up.

LAINIE.   They were not.

WALKER.   They were. I saw tears. Sixty-year-old union guys. Men who've seen every disgusting, pitiful atrocity that ever happened. I bet they haven't cried since the doctor hit 'em. But they cried tonight. For Michael. For you.

LAINIE.   No one has to cry for me.

WALKER.   They *do*. That's the point. That's the power. You have whatever it takes. You have authority. People feel what you say. You can't help it. They look at you, and they trust what you say.

LAINIE.   What if what I say isn't for the best?

WALKER.   They'll believe it anyway. Right now — not a week ago, not a week from now — but *now*, this instant, people believe what you say. They're moved by it. They may even act on it. How do you

36

think things happen in the world? They happen because every once in awhile enormous numbers of people become ready to hear something. And if you've got what they're ready to hear, then you're a very powerful person.

LAINIE. Walker —

WALKER. Use it. You have to use it. You have to push at the ones who are pushing you.

LAINIE. No one's pushing me.

WALKER. Nothing in this world happens because it ought to. You have to push people into it. Right now, you have a quality that lets you push. You have a thing to say, and the means to say it. If you're lucky, when you look back on it, it'll have been moral. If not, too bad — you made your best guess.

LAINIE. When did you first decide I had this . . . quality?

WALKER. First time we talked.

LAINIE. And that's why you've kept at this? With me?

WALKER. Lainie —

LAINIE. I mean it. Is that all this has been? You've just been waiting for me to . . . blossom into some kind of spokesperson for you?

WALKER. Not for me, for yourself. For Michael. How do you think you're going to get him back? ESP? You going to pray he'll show up? He won't. You'll get him back when you make this government uncomfortable enough to make some other government uncomfortable enough to lean on somebody — that's it. *(She stares at her coffee.)*

LAINIE. You'll write a lot of articles now, won't you? No matter how it comes out.

WALKER. Yes, I will. That's my job. That's how I push. *(A beat.)* So look — in my business, when you make the government uncomfortable you drink champagne, not coffee. What do you say? *(He offers her his glass. She doesn't take it.)*

LAINIE. Go home.

WALKER. Go home?

LAINIE. I don't feel like celebrating.

WALKER. Why not?

LAINIE. Because for all I know, I haven't done anything more than risk the lives of innocent people tonight. That's no reason to

37

celebrate.

WALKER. That's not what you were saying earlier.

LAINIE. Earlier I didn't think I was with someone who — *(She stops herself.)*

WALKER. Someone who what? Who what, Lainie?

LAINIE. Who makes friends just so he can . . . push.

WALKER. I have to be able to do my job.

LAINIE. That's what Ellen says. It's probably what the Shi'ites say.

WALKER. What's wrong with that? It's a world of work, Lainie.

LAINIE. It's a world of crime. We call it work so we can keep doing it. *(A beat.)*

WALKER. I'm sorry you feel this way. I think I've been pretty damn patient, all things considered. I've waited a year for a story that —

LAINIE. *Michael's* waiting. Not you. Not me. Michael.

WALKER. *I know! That's why I'm writing about the stupid fuck!!* *(A long beat.)* Lainie? *(A beat. He takes a hesitant step towards her, pulls back.)* I'll call you in the morning. *(He exits quickly U. with the champagne, his glass and her cup. Lainie sits on the mat thoughtfully for a moment, then lies back on it, and closes her eyes. Lights change, isolating her on the mat.)*

LAINIE. Michael? The first time I saw you, time turned a corner. I'd always thought of it as gray, impassive. But it wasn't. When I married you, I felt as though time were our child. That somehow we could . . . *(She stops, sits up.)* We could shape it to our lives. *(Lights fade. In the darkness we hear Walker's voice. When lights rise, Lainie is sitting in a corner on the floor.)*

WALKER. *(Off.)* Lainie? It's me, Walker. Can I come in? *(Off.)* Lainie? *(Off.)* Your car's in the garage; I know you're here. *(Off.)* Lainie? *(After a moment, Walker enters. He looks at Lainie with concern but not surprise.)* It's not a defeat. It's a step closer. *(No response. He moves to her.)* They released Mathison. Plus everybody from the charter terminal. That's a step. They recognized a linkage. They bargained. We can take credit for that. You're as responsible as anyone that Jim Mathison's free now.

LAINIE. Why him?

WALKER. No one knows. *(A beat.)* You haven't been answering your phone.

LAINIE. Reporters call. *(Of the mat.)* I can't see him anymore. All morning I haven't been able to feel him. I can't remember what he looks like.

WALKER.   He'll come back. I know he will. *(She moves to the mat on all fours, places a hand at its center.)*

LAINIE.   He may as well have disappeared into the earth. Right here. On this spot. I would feel more hope.

WALKER.   Lainie, he's . . . For God's sake, we got Mathison back.

LAINIE.   Did you see the President? On the news? "We have them back now, after eight harrowing days of captivity."

WALKER.   *Plus Mathison.*

LAINIE.   Is that what they tell mothers of dead soldiers? "Your boy's dead, but don't worry — the one right next to him was just fine."

WALKER.   I'm just saying that Mathison —

LAINIE.   *I didn't do this for Mathison! HE'S NOT MINE! (A beat. She collapses on the mat, crying. Walker hesitates, moves to the door, stops, moves to her. He strokes her shoulder and arm awkwardly, tenderly. She is on her side, facing away from him. He stares up and away while she cries. As her crying abates, his stroking moves to her hair. After a moment, she moves closer to him, so that her head rests on his lap. She slowly grows silent as he continues to stroke her hair. Lights fade to black. Lights back up on Michael sitting alone on the mat.)*

MICHAEL.   Sometimes I wake up with the most intense desire to know what day it is. Sunday? Thursday? I feel like I'm going to die the next minute if I don't find out. Other times I'll wake up and suddenly realize that months have gone by — must have gone by — since I last had a conscious thought about time. It makes me feel like the astronaut who travels forty years at the speed of light and then returns, no older. "What's happened to everyone?" he must think. "Time must be for them, not me." I never thought of time as a coat you could take off and put on again. Too cold to live without it — so we all keep it on. We hug it to ourselves, because if we can't . . . *(A beat.)* Time is change. That's all it is. When there's no change. When there's no change . . . Yesterday one of my guards told me I'd been here three years. *(A beat.)* I didn't know what he meant. *(Lights fade to black.)*

Scene Three

Lights rise on Ellen, sitting on the ottoman. The window is open.

LAINIE. *(Off.)* Oh — Darjeeling or English Breakfast? I can't remember.

ELLEN. English Breakfast. Always.

LAINIE. *(Entering with the tray-table and tea.)* Good. That's what I made. Imagine me forgetting. *(She sets down the tray-table and pours tea for them both.)* How've you been?

ELLEN. Fine. Just got back from a vacation, actually.

LAINIE. Really? Where'd you go?

ELLEN. St. Thomas.

LAINIE. You went there last year, didn't you?

ELLEN. It's where I go every year. I even go to the same hotel there every year. It's the one my husband and I used to stay in when we were married. We both still go there. Only he goes a month before I do now.

LAINIE. That's an interesting arrangement.

ELLEN. It's not an arrangement at all. It's a circumstance. *(A beat.)* How are you holding up?

LAINIE. About the same. It's been a long time.

ELLEN. We're aware of that —

LAINIE. Since I've seen you, I mean.

ELLEN. Yes, well —

LAINIE. I've just gone back to work.

ELLEN. Really?

LAINIE. Last month. I'm teaching again. Everyone there is being very considerate. No "What's it like?" questions.

ELLEN. Good.

LAINIE. Strange to be around so many people all day. I'd gotten out of the habit. *(A beat.)* Have you heard anything new about Michael?

ELLEN. Not specifically —

LAINIE. I thought when you called —

ELLEN. No, it wasn't that we'd heard anything new about Michael, precisely.

40

LAINIE. What was it then?

ELLEN. Nothing, actually, Nothing official.

LAINIE. Is there something you want to say to me?

ELLEN. Of course. I'm here, aren't I?

LAINIE. Then why don't you say it?

ELLEN. It's just a little tricky, to be frank. It's — well, I'd like to feel I'm not here in my official capacity this time. That is, if you could feel that way.

LAINIE. Why?

ELLEN. Could you feel that way? *(A beat.)*

LAINIE. All right.

ELLEN. Good. I wanted to tell you about something that happened last night. It, um — well, it certainly took me by surprise.

LAINIE. What happened?

ELLEN. We intercepted someone. A terrorist. Not a Shi'ite, not even Lebanese. But an Arab, and . . . we killed him.

LAINIE. You what?

ELLEN. He fought back. He resisted. It made no sense — he was completely surrounded, but . . . he resisted.

LAINIE. Where?

ELLEN. In a small Italian coastal town. It should be on the news within an hour or so. We've managed to hold it back a bit, but —

LAINIE. What are you saying?

ELLEN. I think you know what I'm saying.

LAINIE. Michael's in more danger now?

ELLEN. They all are. *(A beat.)* It was bad enough for Michael that we intercepted this man. But to kill him. I'm afraid it's a very dangerous situation.

LAINIE. Not for you.

ELLEN. Lainie —

LAINIE. Whose idea was this?

ELLEN. I couldn't tell you if I knew.

LAINIE. What was the point? What did you think you had to gain?

ELLEN. This man was implicated in the deaths of scores of American citizens. He was behind at least three bombings.

LAINIE. So somebody at State said, "Kill him."

ELLEN. They *did not*. They decided to capture him. If possible.

LAINIE. And it wasn't. So now Michael's going to —

ELLEN. Nothing will happen to Michael, for all we know. The risks were carefully analyzed, and —

LAINIE. The President's image — that's what was analyzed. Did he need to look forceful this week?

ELLEN. We can't assume that any of the hostages will be harmed simply because one terrorist leader was intercepted.

LAINIE. Killed! Use English! *(A beat.)*

ELLEN. Killed. It was the judgment of the Department that Michael and the others would not be overly . . . endangered.

LAINIE. Was that your judgment? *(A beat.)* You never answer questions like that, do you?

ELLEN. No.

LAINIE. Is it because you know if you started you'd never be able to stop? *(A beat.)*

ELLEN. Early in the war between Iran and Iraq, there was an offensive. Iranian soldiers — Shi'ites, like the people holding Michael — needed a way to break through Iraqi minefields. They chose and all-out frontal assault, classic World War I stuff. But with one difference. To clear the mine fields, the Iranian army — which has some significant technical limitations — used boys. The boys didn't go out and dig up the mines. They ran over them. The mines blew up, killing the boys, and the soldiers followed after, across the newly-cleared fields. These boys were fourteen, fifteen — up to twenty. Some were as young as ten. They had . . . volunteered for the duty. They wanted to be martyrs. And their families too, many of them, freely gave their sons to this honor. The boys wore white headbands, ran into the fields shouting "Shaheed", which means martyr. Some of them wrapped themselves in blankets first, so that when they were killed the explosions wouldn't blow them apart quite so much, and their bodies could be . . . gathered more easily, and returned home to inspire other boys to take the same path. Their parents do not grieve. They are proud, and satisfied their sons are in heaven — to them a place as tangible as this, without pain. *(A beat.)* There are times when it becomes impossible to negotiate. When the very act of negotiating legitimizes a philosophy that's . . . not human anymore. Those places where such a philosophy reigns have to be isolated. Those people who try to extend such a philosophy must be stopped. At any cost.

42

LAINIE. Any cost?

ELLEN. Any cost. *(Lights fade to black. They come up quickly again on Lainie and Walker. Lainie is very agitated.)*

WALKER. I don't think it means anything.

LAINIE. What do you mean, it doesn't mean anything? They said they were going to kill him!

WALKER. It's a radio report. They've been wrong dozens of times. They're almost never right.

LAINIE. What if they're right this time?

WALKER. It's a tactic. That's all it is. We hit them, they threaten the hostages. Nothing happens. It's just a pressure game.

LAINIE. This isn't a threat. They said they were going to kill him.

WALKER. That announcement didn't even come from his captors. It came from an entirely different faction. They wouldn't even know where he is, let alone how he is.

LAINIE. Oh, God — I can't stand this. I can't. Not knowing — this is . . . oh, *GOD!!*

WALKER. Lainie — *(She moves away from him, pacing the room with increasing agitation.)*

LAINIE. There is a circle of hell for these people. There is a circle of hell so deep —

WALKER. Lainie, calm down —

LAINIE. *NO!!*

WALKER. You know, there might even be an advantage in this.

LAINIE. Advantage!!

WALKER. Listen to me! A false story's been broadcast. Michael's kidnappers may have to show pictures of him alive now. There could be a video tape, or —

LAINIE. And if there's nothing?

WALKER. That doesn't mean anything either. They can play this a lot of different ways. The point is, they've kept him for three years. And now they're just going to kill him? When they've got nothing to gain? It's not rational.

LAINIE. What's rational about killing? *(A beat.)* I want to go on TV. I want to talk to somebody. To everybody. I want to —

WALKER. You shouldn't do that.

LAINIE. Why not?!

WALKER. Nothing's known yet. We have to wait and find out the status of things.

LAINIE. *Status!?*

WALKER. We killed one of their people. I don't think Michael's captors want to hear from any American right now — even you.

LAINIE. I didn't kill anyone.

WALKER. *We* did. The country did. We have to wait for some time to pass.

LAINIE. How am I supposed to sleep? Till we hear. How am I supposed to live? Not knowing.

WALKER. I don't know. But that's the situation we're in. They can say he's alive, they can say he's dead —

LAINIE. They can say *anything!* They can do *anything* . . . to him. *(A beat.)* We should obliterate the city.

WALKER. Lainie —

LAINIE. Why not!!? Don't you want to!? Lebanon, the Middle East — let's *get rid of it! (Walker grabs Lainie and hugs her to him tight.)* I want to kill them.

WALKER. It's all right.

LAINIE. I want to kill them.

WALKER. I know. It's all right.

LAINIE. I want to kill a million people. *(He continues to hold her. Reluctantly, her arms finally go around him. They freeze in this position. Michael enters — handcuffs, no blindfold. He circles them as he speaks, but doesn't look at them. He finishes his speech staring out the window.)*

MICHAEL. One night someone came to move me. It was no one I knew — none of my guards. I was blindfolded, but I could tell by his voice. He spoke English better than any of them. He said I had to be moved at once — that the Syrian Army might have learned where I was. He was nervous, but there was a softness in his voice, too. I think he was young. *(A beat.)* Some clothes were thrown on me and I was hustled into the back seat of a car by three men. All the voices were new — not one of them was familiar. It was actually a cool night. The feeling of being outside was incredible. I listened for anything — any sound, any voice — over the noise of the car. Not because I was planning to escape. Just for the sheer, sensual pleasure of it. A sound, at random. A voice. Anything that was completely disconnected from my being a hostage. That just . . . existed in the world. And I thought for some reason about all the things that always exist in the world simultaneously — with or without us. Innumerable parts of a system designed to not even recognize itself as a system. Dogs barking in the streets, wind in the shop awnings, people talking on corners, flowers letting go their fragrance, people riding bicycles, pigeons mourning nobody we know, people driving in cars, people buying oranges, distant explosions, people carrying guns, people dying of poison gas, oceans rocking on their stems, people making love for the first time in their lives, people designing clothes-hangers, people designing the end of the world, people in movie theaters, people singing in languages we don't understand, insects filling the world — *filling* the world — people in restaurants ordering the best meal of their lives, people using the phone, petting their cats, holding each other in each other's arms. *(A beat.)* All of it, at once. *(A beat.)* They drove me to a quiet neighborhood and shoved me into a building. I was taken down, still blindfolded, to a small, cramped room that smelled like . . . clay, and I was shot to death. *(Michael exits, but not U. He passes through the 'wall' of the room. Lights fade to black.)*

Scene Four

Lights rise. The room is empty. Walker enters carrying the chair. He sets it down. Ellen appears at the door.

ELLEN.   Do we have to be in here?

WALKER.   That's what she wants. *(A beat.)*

ELLEN.   There are three reporters outside. They seemed to know I was coming. Did you tell them?

WALKER.   Not me. I like exclusives. Maybe they're just here because it's an important story. Then again, maybe they like watching the State Department deal with the consequences. *(A beat.)* So, when's the phone call from the President?

ELLEN.   He's sending a letter.

WALKER.   A letter? No post-game phone call? No national hookup?

ELLEN.   Not this time.

WALKER.   Have you done a lot of this kind of work? Bearer of ill-tidings?

ELLEN. Some. When I worked in the Defense Department.

WALKER. Now there's a job.

ELLEN. It's nothing one looks forward to.

WALKER. What did you say to them?

ELLEN. What can you say? I told them their men were heroes. I said, "Your husband, son, brother, father was a hero. He died of bad luck." Not bad planning at the top, not tactical mistakes of his commanders. Bad luck.

WALKER. And they believed you?

ELLEN. Oh, yes. *(A beat. He looks out the window.)*

WALKER. Is that what you're going to tell Lainie? That Michael died of bad luck?

ELLEN. No, Lainie gets the truth.

WALKER. Which is?

ELLEN. Off the record?

WALKER. Nothing's off the record. *(Ellen shrugs, sits silently. Walker sighs and looks out the window.)* All right, all right — off the record. *(As Ellen speaks, Lainie enters silently U. Neither of them sees her.)*

ELLEN. We miscalculated. We valued Michael's life below a chance to make an international point. We increased the danger for all the hostages. We chose to.

LAINIE. Thank you. *(They turn with surprise.)*

ELLEN. Lainie, I . . . I wasn't —

LAINIE. Going to say it like that? I'm glad you did. *(A beat.)* Is that all your business?

ELLEN. The President is sending you a letter.

LAINIE. I'll burn it.

ELLEN. Your husband's remains will arrive tomorrow morning at Andrews Air Force base. If you have no objections, there will be a short ceremony —

LAINIE. I object.

ELLEN. The body will be transported at government expense to a funeral home of your choice.

LAINIE. I get a choice?

ELLEN. Simply inform us where. *(A beat.)* Allow me to take this opportunity to convey the deep sympathy of the Secretary of State.

LAINIE. Go to hell.

ELLEN. And the President.

LAINIE. Why are you saying this?!

ELLEN. It's my job to say this.

LAINIE. You don't have a job. You have a license to manipulate. *(A beat.)* I want to be like you. Tell me how to be like you.

ELLEN. What do you mean?

LAINIE. I want to think like you. I want to be able to put people away, in my head. I want to forget them there. I want to lock them in whatever room you have for that.

WALKER. Lainie —

LAINIE. Teach me! *(A beat.)* You won't, will you? That's your most closely-guarded secret. That's where all the real weapons are.

WALKER. *(To Ellen.)* You should go.

LAINIE. No. Not till I say. Ellen, I think you and government did your best. I think everyone did his best. Michael did his best, Walker did his best, you did, the Shi'ites — even the ones that killed Michael. Probably everyone has done his best. That's what frightens me. That's why I don't know if I'll ever be able to walk out of this room anymore. Into what? A world filled with people doing their best?

ELLEN. I wish I could take your pain away.

LAINIE. I wish you could remember it. *(Ellen exits U. A beat.)*

WALKER. Do you need me to be here?

LAINIE. Not right now. Not for awhile.

WALKER. I'd like to be.

LAINIE. No.

WALKER. Why not? *(A beat.)* I don't think you should be alone.

LAINIE. I'm not. *(A beat.)*

WALKER. What about tomorrow? I'll drive you to the Air Force base.

LAINIE. Thank you. You should go now.

WALKER. Are you sure? *(She nods, stares at the mat. He looks around the room.)* I'll call you later. All right? Lainie? *(A beat.)* Lainie? *(She moves to the mat, kneels down beside it, stares at it. Walker studies her for a moment, then starts out U.)*

LAINIE. *(Pointing at the chair.)* Could you take that out? Too much furniture. *(Walker picks it up, stares at her, then leaves. She is again focussed on the mat. Her hand strokes through the air, as though caressing Michael's face. At this point Michael enters U., silently. He moves to the mat and reclines on it, so that her hand now strokes his hair.)* I think my favorite is the African hornbill.

MICHAEL.   Of all birds. Why?

LAINIE.   After they mate, the male walls the female up, in the hollow of a tree. He literally imprisons her. And all through the weeks of incubating the eggs, he flies off and finds food, and brings it back and feeds her — through a little hole in the wall he's built. After the eggs are hatched, he breaks down the wall again, and the whole family is united for the first time. You see? It hasn't been a prison at all. It's been . . . a fortress.

MICHAEL.   Their devotion, you mean?

LAINIE.   Their devotion. *(He smiles, closes his eyes. She continues to stroke his hair. Lights fade to black.)*

THE END

Property List

Narrow floor mat
Handcuffs
Blindfold
Small ottoman
Small tray table
Tea set
Tea
Chair
Photograph
Glass of champagne
Cup of coffee

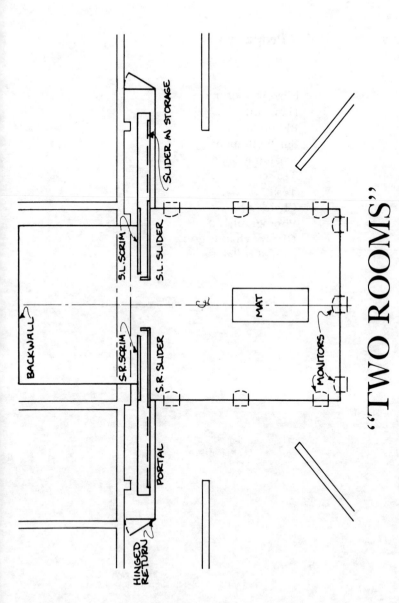

"TWO ROOMS"

Designed by Marjorie Bradley Kellogg for the La Jolla Playhouse production.

NEW PLAYS

★ **THE EXONERATED by Jessica Blank and Erik Jensen.** Six interwoven stories paint a picture of an American criminal justice system gone horribly wrong and six brave souls who persevered to survive it. "The #1 play of the year...intense and deeply affecting..." *–NY Times.* "Riveting. Simple, honest storytelling that demands reflection." *–A.P.* "Artful and moving...pays tribute to the resilience of human hearts and minds." *–Variety.* "Stark...riveting...cunningly orchestrated." *–The New Yorker.* "Hard-hitting, powerful, and socially relevant." *–Hollywood Reporter.* [7M, 3W] ISBN: 0-8222-1946-8

★ **STRING FEVER by Jacquelyn Reingold.** Lily juggles the big issues: turning forty, artificial insemination and the elusive scientific Theory of Everything in this Off-Broadway comedy hit. "Applies the elusive rules of string theory to the conundrums of one woman's love life. Think *Sex and the City* meets *Copenhagen*." *–NY Times.* "A funny offbeat and touching look at relationships...an appealing romantic comedy populated by oddball characters." *–NY Daily News.* "Where kooky, zany, and madcap meet...whimsically winsome." *–NY Magazine.* "STRING FEVER will have audience members happily stringing along." *–TheaterMania.com.* "Reingold's language is surprising, inventive, and unique." *–nytheatre.com.* "...[a] whimsical comic voice." *–Time Out.* [3M, 3W (doubling)] ISBN: 0-8222-1952-2

★ **DEBBIE DOES DALLAS adapted by Erica Schmidt, composed by Andrew Sherman, conceived by Susan L. Schwartz.** A modern morality tale told as a comic musical of tragic proportions as the classic film is brought to the stage. "A scream! A saucy, tongue-in-cheek romp." *–The New Yorker.* "Hilarious! DEBBIE manages to have it all: beauty, brains and a great sense of humor!" *–Time Out.* "Shamelessly silly, shrewdly self-aware and proud of being naughty. Great fun!" *–NY Times.* "Racy and raucous, a lighthearted, fast-paced thoroughly engaging and hilarious send-up." *–NY Daily News.* [3M, 5W] ISBN: 0-8222-1955-7

★ **THE MYSTERY PLAYS by Roberto Aguirre-Sacasa.** Two interrelated one acts, loosely based on the tradition of the medieval mystery plays. "... stylish, spine-tingling...Mr. Aguirre-Sacasa uses standard tricks of horror stories, borrowing liberally from masters like Kafka, Lovecraft, Hitchock...But his mastery of the genre is his own...irresistible." *–NY Times.* "Undaunted by the special-effects limitations of theatre, playwright and *Marvel* comicbook writer Roberto Aguirre-Sacasa maps out some creepy twilight zones in THE MYSTERY PLAYS, an engaging, related pair of one acts...The theatre may rarely deliver shocks equivalent to, say, *Dawn of the Dead*, but Aguirre-Sacasa's work is fine compensation." *–Time Out.* [4M, 2W] ISBN: 0-8222-2038-5

★ **THE JOURNALS OF MIHAIL SEBASTIAN by David Auburn.** This epic one-man play spans eight tumultuous years and opens a uniquely personal window on the Romanian Holocaust and the Second World War. "Powerful." *–NY Times.* "[THE JOURNALS OF MIHAIL SEBASTIAN] allows us to glimpse the idiosyncratic effects of that awful history on one intelligent, pragmatic, recognizably real man..." *–NY Newsday.* [3M, 5W] ISBN: 0-8222-2006-7

★ **LIVING OUT by Lisa Loomer.** The story of the complicated relationship between a Salvadoran nanny and the Anglo lawyer she works for. "A stellar new play. Searingly funny." *–The New Yorker.* "Both generous and merciless, equally enjoyable and disturbing." *–NY Newsday.* "A bitingly funny new comedy. The plight of working mothers is explored from two pointedly contrasting perspectives in this sympathetic, sensitive new play." *–Variety.* [2M, 6W] ISBN: 0-8222-1994-8

DRAMATISTS PLAY SERVICE, INC.
440 Park Avenue South, New York, NY 10016 212-683-8960 Fax 212-213-1539
postmaster@dramatists.com www.dramatists.com

NEW PLAYS

★ **MATCH by Stephen Belber.** Mike and Lisa Davis interview a dancer and choreographer about his life, but it is soon evident that their agenda will either ruin or inspire them—and definitely change their lives forever. "Prolific laughs and ear-to-ear smiles." *–NY Magazine.* "Uproariously funny, deeply moving, enthralling theater. Stephen Belber's MATCH has great beauty and tenderness, and abounds in wit." *–NY Daily News.* "Three and a half out of four stars." *–USA Today.* "A theatrical steeplechase that leads straight from outrageous bitchery to unadorned, heartfelt emotion." *–Wall Street Journal.* [2M, 1W] ISBN: 0-8222-2020-2

★ **HANK WILLIAMS: LOST HIGHWAY by Randal Myler and Mark Harelik.** The story of the beloved and volatile country-music legend Hank Williams, featuring twenty-five of his most unforgettable songs. "[LOST HIGHWAY has] the exhilarating feeling of Williams on stage in a particular place on a particular night…serves up classic country with the edges raw and the energy hot…By the end of the play, you've traveled on a profound emotional journey: LOST HIGHWAY transports its audience and communicates the inspiring message of the beauty and richness of Williams' songs…forceful, clear-eyed, moving, impressive." *–Rolling Stone.* "…honors a very particular musical talent with care and energy… smart, sweet, poignant." *–NY Times.* [7M, 3W] ISBN: 0-8222-1985-9

★ **THE STORY by Tracey Scott Wilson.** An ambitious black newspaper reporter goes against her editor to investigate a murder and finds the *best* story…but at what cost? "A singular new voice…deeply emotional, deeply intellectual, and deeply musical…" *–The New Yorker.* "…a conscientious and absorbing new drama…" *–NY Times.* "…a riveting, tough-minded drama about race, reporting and the truth…" *–A.P.* "… a stylish, attention-holding script that ends on a chilling note that will leave viewers with much to talk about." *–Curtain Up.* [2M, 7W (doubling, flexible casting)] ISBN: 0-8222-1998-0

★ **OUR LADY OF 121st STREET by Stephen Adly Guirgis.** The body of Sister Rose, beloved Harlem nun, has been stolen, reuniting a group of life-challenged childhood friends who square off as they wait for her return. "A scorching and dark new comedy…" Mr. Guirgis has one of the finest imaginations for dialogue to come along in years." *–NY Times.* "Stephen Guirgis may be the best playwright in America under forty." *–NY Magazine.* [8M, 4W] ISBN: 0-8222-1965-4

★ **HOLLYWOOD ARMS by Carrie Hamilton and Carol Burnett.** The coming-of-age story of a dreamer who manages to escape her bleak life and follow her romantic ambitions to stardom. Based on Carol Burnett's bestselling autobiography, *One More Time.* "…pure theatre and pure entertainment…" *–Talkin' Broadway.* "…a warm, fuzzy evening of theatre." *–BrodwayBeat.com.* "…chuckles and smiles of recognition or surprise flow naturally…a remarkable slice of life." *–TheatreScene.net.* [5M, 5W, 1 girl] ISBN: 0-8222-1959-X

★ **INVENTING VAN GOGH by Steven Dietz.** A haunting and hallucinatory drama about the making of art, the obsession to create and the fine line that separates truth from myth. "Like a van Gogh painting, Dietz's story is a gorgeous example of excess—one that remakes reality with broad, well-chosen brush strokes. At evening's end, we're left with the author's resounding opinions on art and artifice, and provoked by his constant query into which is greater: van Gogh's art or his violent myth." *–Phoenix New Times.* "Dietz's writing is never simple. It is always brilliant. Shaded, compressed, direct, lucid—he frames his subject with a remarkable understanding of painting as a physical experience." *–Tucson Citizen.* [4M, 1W] ISBN: 0-8222-1954-9

DRAMATISTS PLAY SERVICE, INC.
440 Park Avenue South, New York, NY 10016   212-683-8960   Fax 212-213-1539
postmaster@dramatists.com   www.dramatists.com

NEW PLAYS

★ **INTIMATE APPAREL by Lynn Nottage.** The moving and lyrical story of a turn-of-the-century black seamstress whose gifted hands and sewing machine are the tools she uses to fashion her dreams from the whole cloth of her life's experiences. "...Nottage's play has a delicacy and eloquence that seem absolutely right for the time she is depicting..." *–NY Daily News.* "...thoughtful, affecting...The play offers poignant commentary on an era when the cut and color of one's dress—and of course, skin—determined whom one could and could not marry, sleep with, even talk to in public." *–Variety.* [2M, 4W] ISBN: 0-8222-2009-1

★ **BROOKLYN BOY by Donald Margulies.** A witty and insightful look at what happens to a writer when his novel hits the bestseller list. "The characters are beautifully drawn, the dialogue sparkles..." *–nytheatre.com.* "Few playwrights have the mastery to smartly investigate so much through a laugh-out-loud comedy that combines the vintage subject matter of successful writer-returning-to-ethnic-roots with the familiar mid-life crisis." *–Show Business Weekly.* [4M, 3W] ISBN: 0-8222-2074-1

★ **CROWNS by Regina Taylor.** Hats become a springboard for an exploration of black history and identity in this celebratory musical play. "Taylor pulls off a Hat Trick: She scores thrice, turning CROWNS into an artful amalgamation of oral history, fashion show, and musical theater..." *–TheatreMania.com.* "...wholly theatrical...Ms. Taylor has created a show that seems to arise out of spontaneous combustion, as if a bevy of department-store customers simultaneously decided to stage a revival meeting in the changing room." *–NY Times.* [1M, 6W (2 musicians)] ISBN: 0-8222-1963-8

★ **EXITS AND ENTRANCES by Athol Fugard.** The story of a relationship between a young playwright on the threshold of his career and an aging actor who has reached the end of his. "[Fugard] can say more with a single line than most playwrights convey in an entire script...Paraphrasing the title, it's safe to say this drama, making its memorable entrance into our consciousness, is unlikely to exit as long as a theater exists for exceptional work." *–Variety.* "A thought-provoking, elegant and engrossing new play..." *–Hollywood Reporter.* [2M] ISBN: 0-8222-2041-5

★ **BUG by Tracy Letts.** A thriller featuring a pair of star-crossed lovers in an Oklahoma City motel facing a bug invasion, paranoia, conspiracy theories and twisted psychological motives. "...obscenely exciting...top-flight craftsmanship. Buckle up and brace yourself..." *–NY Times.* "...[a] thoroughly outrageous and thoroughly entertaining play...the possibility of enemies, real and imagined, to squash has never been more theatrical." *–A.P.* [3M, 2W] ISBN: 0-8222-2016-4

★ **THOM PAIN (BASED ON NOTHING) by Will Eno.** An ordinary man muses on childhood, yearning, disappointment and loss, as he draws the audience into his last-ditch plea for empathy and enlightenment. "It's one of those treasured nights in the theater—treasured nights anywhere, for that matter—that can leave you both breathless with exhilaration and...in a puddle of tears." *–NY Times.* "Eno's words...are familiar, but proffered in a way that is constantly contradictory to our expectations. Beckett is certainly among his literary ancestors." *–nytheatre.com.* [1M] ISBN: 0-8222-2076-8

★ **THE LONG CHRISTMAS RIDE HOME by Paula Vogel.** Past, present and future collide on a snowy Christmas Eve for a troubled family of five. "...[a] lovely and hauntingly original family drama...a work that breathes so much life into the theater." *–Time Out.* "...[a] delicate visual feast..." *–NY Times.* "...brutal and lovely...the overall effect is magical." *–NY Newsday.* [3M, 3W] ISBN: 0-8222-2003-2

DRAMATISTS PLAY SERVICE, INC.
440 Park Avenue South, New York, NY 10016 212-683-8960 Fax 212-213-1539
postmaster@dramatists.com www.dramatists.com